Introduction

Presenting Poetry provides the basis of a number of poetry sessions for primary classes (approximately 8- to 12-year-olds). The units contain:
1. a group of poems linked by a common theme, structure or feature;
2. some questions about the poems, designed to help pupils get the most out of their reading;
3. one or more follow-up activities, for example art or craft work, drama, discussion, music, recitation, choral presentation or poetry writing. These activities are often non-written and intended to show poetry as linked to the aesthetic and expressive arts.

A typical poetry session might take the following shape:
1. re-reading together of a poem or poems enjoyed in a previous session;
2. time for pupils to choose and read for pleasure, with the group, some of their favourite poems;
3. a detailed look at one unit, and follow-up work related to it. The book can, of course, also be used more informally in odd moments as a poetry anthology.

Reading the poems

When pupils meet each poem for the first time, it should be through the teacher's reading, because a well-read rendering maximises the listener's pleasure. It is strongly recommended, therefore, that teachers *practise* each poem before reading it aloud for the first time to the class. Later on, the pupils should have an opportunity to read aloud themselves. If the teacher has provided a good example of how to handle rhythm, rhyme, dramatic effects, etc., the pupil's task will be easier and more pleasurable. The pupil will also have been introduced to new or difficult words or ideas.

After this first teacher-reading of the poem, the pupil's understanding should be ensured through discussion based on the comprehension questions in the text. A second teacher-reading of the poem is often a good idea, before handing over to pupil-readers.

Although comprehension questions are included, full comprehension by all pupils of all poems is not always possible – nor is it essential. Children are well used to coping with half-grasped ideas, and may enjoy the sounds and images of the more difficult poems for their own sake.

It is recommended that all pupil-readers be volunteers and that no pupil be forced to read. It is best to choose competent volunteers first and less competent ones later on when they have had a chance to become more familiar with words and rhythms from several hearings. It is worth trying a wide range of reading methods: single voice reading, paired reading, group reading, choral reading, and combinations of these. Happy chanting (where appropriate) is not to be despised: it gives pleasure and helps commit poems to memory. When possible and practical, children may be encouraged to use sound effects, music, etc., to accompany their readings.

Follow-up

Any follow-up work should be varied and pleasurable. Some poetry writing is included as part of a balanced follow-up programme. Unit poems are often used as a model for the pupil's work, since this is an effective way of starting children off on their own poetry writing. Learning poetry by heart is a useful memory-training exercise and can provide great pleasure. Children should be encouraged to learn their favourite poems by heart every now and then. Often poems are picked up effortlessly if they are read aloud frequently. The prospect of an audience motivates children's performance enormously. Try to provide an audience – another class, the school – for their presentations.

Contents

Hurry, Hurry

Have you ever noticed how grown-ups are always trying to hurry children? When you are playing they often decide it is time for you do something else.
When has this happened to you?
The first poem in this unit is about being rushed off to bed before you want to go.

Bedtime

Five minutes, five minutes more, please!
    Let me stay five minutes more!
Can't I just finish the castle
    I'm building here on the floor?
Can't I just finish the story
    I'm reading here in my book?
Can't I just finish this bead-chain—
    It *almost* is finished, look!
Can't I just finish this game, please?
    When a game's once begun
It's a pity never to find out
    Whether you've lost or won.
Can't I just stay five minutes?
    Well, can't I stay just four?
Three minutes, then? two minutes?
    Can't I stay *one* minute more?

Eleanor Farjeon

What is your bedtime? Do you want to go to bed at this time?
Why or why not?
Have you any good ways of avoiding being sent to bed?
Grown-ups sometimes try sneaky tricks to hurry you. The grown-up in the next poem wants the child to be ready by the count of fifteen.
When the grown-up is speaking, the line begins nearer the edge of the page. When the child is speaking the line starts further in.

One, Two, Three

If you don't put your shoes on before I count fifteen then
we won't go to the woods to climb the chestnut, one
   But I can't find them.
Two.
   I can't
They're under the sofa, three
   No. O yes
Four five six
   Stop—they've got knots they've got knots
You should untie the laces when you take your shoes off, seven
   Will you do one shoe while I do the other then?
Eight, but that would be cheating
   Please
All right
   It always . . .
Nine
   It always sticks—I'll use my teeth
Ten
   It won't it won't. It has—look
Eleven
   I'm not wearing any socks.
Twelve
   Stop counting stop counting. Mum, where are my socks, mum?
They're in your shoes. Where you left them.
   I didn't.
Thirteen
   O, they're inside out and upside down and bundled up
Fourteen
   Have you done the knot on the shoe you were . . .
Yes, put it on the right foot
   But socks don't have a right and wrong foot

The shoes silly. Fourteen and a half.
  I am I am. Wait
  Don't go to the woods without me
  Look that's one shoe already
Fourteen and three quarters
  There
You haven't tied the bows yet
  We could do them on the way there
No we won't. Fourteen and seven eighths
  Help me then.
  You know I'm not fast at bows
Fourteen and fifteen sixteeeenths
  A single bow is alright isn't it?
Fifteen. We're off.
  See I did it.
  Didn't I?

Michael Rosen

Do you know any adults who use this trick?
Does it usually work? Why or why not?
What other tricks do adults use to get you to
hurry?
One of the things that makes grown-ups cross
is being kept waiting — like the mother in the
next poem.

Hurry Home

You had better hurry home for your supper's nearly
  ready,
Your mother's in the kitchen and she's awfully wild,
She's been shouting at the cat, and she keeps on
  saying,
"O where has he got to, the wretched child?"

She has been to the front door and looked through
  the window
And now she's banging on the frying pan,
The plates and the dishes are all on the table,
So run, my boy, as fast as you can.

Don't you know she's cooking your favourite supper,
Potatoes in their jackets and beefsteak pie?
She's made a jug of custard for the pudding in the
  oven,
Get a move on, Joe, the stars are in the sky.

They've all left the factory, the streets will soon be
  empty,
No more playing now, it's time you fed,
It really is a shame to keep your mother waiting,
So come have your supper, and then off to bed.

Leonard Clark

What clues in this poem show that Joe's mum
is cross and getting crosser?
Why is she cross? Try to think of more than
one reason.
If you were Joe would you be looking forward
to getting home? Why?

Do you have a set time for coming home in
the evening? Is it the same time in the summer
as in winter?
Do you think grown-ups are right to want
children to come inside when it's dark? Would
you rather be allowed to play outside all night?

ACTIVITY: **Reading Poems**

1. Let some people try reading *Bedtime* in the
   right kind of voice. It should be a begging,
   pleading voice. It should build up and up to
   the last line, sounding more desperate all
   the time.
2. Let some pairs of people try reading *One,
   Two, Three*. The person being the mum
   must sound very patient but very firm. The
   person being the child is in a muddle, and
   must plead and panic. At the end, however,
   the child's voice should change.
3. *Hurry Home* is a poem with a strong
   rhythm. Practise tapping it out with a pencil
   while your teacher reads the poem again.
   Now let some people read a verse each. Try
   tapping while they read. This helps you get
   the right rhythm.
Try to make your voice go up at the end of
any questions. Be sure to sound really cross
and worried for "O where has he got to, the
wretched child?"

Now that you have read these poems a few
times, which one do you like best? Why?

UNIT TWO

Monday Tuesday Wednesday Thursday Friday Saturday Sunday

Here is an old rhyme about the days of the week:

Monday's child is fair of face,
Tuesday's child is full of grace,
Wednesday's child is full of woe,
Thursday's child has far to go,
Friday's child is loving and giving,
Saturday's child works hard for his living,
And the child that is born on the Sabbath day
Is bonny and blithe, and good and gay.

What is "the Sabbath day"?
Do you know which day of the week you were born on?
Which day sounds the nicest to be born on?
Which sounds the nastiest?
Do you think the rhyme is true?
Split the rhyme up between seven readers, one for each day of the week. They should try to read their lines in a voice to match the words.

Here is another rhyme about the days of the week:

Sneeze on Monday, sneeze for danger;
Sneeze on Tuesday, kiss a stranger;
Sneeze on Wednesday, get a letter;
Sneeze on Thursday, something better;
Sneeze on Friday, sneeze for sorrow;
Sneeze on Saturday, see your sweetheart
  tomorrow.

So watch out when you sneeze!

The next poem tells how a boy hates a certain day.

Bus to School

Rounding a corner
It comes to a stay.
Quick! Grab the rail!
Now we're off on our way . . .
Oh, but it's Thursday
The day of fear!
Three hateful lessons!
And school draws near.
Here in the 'bus though
There's plenty to see:
Boys full of talk about
Last night's TV;
Girls with their violins,
Armfuls of twigs
And flowers for teacher;
Bartlett and Biggs;

Conductor who chats with them,
Jokes about cricket;
Machine that flicks out
A white ribbon of ticket . . .
Yes, but it's Thursday,
The day of fear!—
Six hateful lessons!
And school draws near.
Conductor now waiting
Firm as a rock,
For Billy whose penny's
Slid down in his sock.
Conductor frowning,
With finger on handle;
Poor Billy blushes,
Undoes his sandal . . .
'Hold very tight, please!
Any more fares?'
Whistling conductor
Goes clumping upstairs . . .
Boots up above now!
Boys coming down! . . .
Over the hump-bridge
And into the town.
Old Warren sweeping
In his shirt-sleeves!
Sun on his shop-front,
Sun on the leaves . . .
Only, it's Thursday,
The day of fear!—
All hateful lessons!
And school draws near.

John Walsh

As the boy gets nearer to school, the thought
of Thursday gets worse. How can you tell?
Two of the words in the poem are printed in
a different way from the others. This sort of
printing is called *italics*.
Why do you think these two words are in
italic print?
Try reading the poem again. Eleven people can
take four lines each, and the whole class can
join in for the last four lines. Put a lot of
feeling into the words in italics.
Which day of the week do *you* hate most?
Which do you like most? Why?

ACTIVITY 1: **An Acrostic Poem**

An acrostic poem uses the first letters of a word, like this:

> Mum's collecting the washing . . .
> Oh no! It's back to school—
> No lie-in today.
> Dreaded Monday,
> A new week ahead . . .
> Yawn!

Can you see the word "Monday" down the left-hand side of the poem?
With your teacher, choose another day of the week. Talk about it first. Then try an acrostic poem.
All work together, and your teacher can write the poem on the board as you make it up.
It does not have to rhyme!

ACTIVITY 2: **The Work of Each Day**

> Wash on Monday,
> Iron on Tuesday,
> Mend on Wednesday,
> Churn on Thursday,
> Clean on Friday,
> Bake on Saturday,
> Rest on Sunday.

In the past, housewives had a different job to do each day. The old rhyme shows one weekly routine.

You might have a weekly routine too. Copy the timetable given on this page on to a piece of paper, and fill in what *you* do on each day of the week.

	MORNING	AFTERNOON	EVENING
MONDAY			
TUESDAY			
WEDNESDAY			
THURSDAY			
FRIDAY			
SATURDAY			
SUNDAY			

UNIT THREE

Strange and Scrumptious

Sweet Song

This is the sweet song,
Song of all the sweets,
Caramel and butterscotch
Bullseyes, raspberry treats;

Treacle toffee, acid drops,
Pastilles, crystal fruits,
Bubble-gum and liquorice-sticks
As black as new gum-boots;

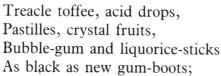

Peppermint creams and aniseed balls,
Tiny sweets and whoppers,
Dolly-mixtures, chocolate drops,
Gigantic gob-stoppers;

Which of the sweets mentioned in the poem
have *you* eaten?
Which is your favourite?
Try miming eating some of the sweets in the
poem, as your teacher reads it again. Don't
forget to mime the tooth and bellyache as
well!
Sweets are bad for your teeth. Should children
be allowed to eat them?

Lemon sherberts, jelly babies,
Chocolate cream and flake,
Nougat, fudge and such as give
You tooth and belly-ache.

Vernon Scannell

This poem is fun to read aloud:

Beautiful Soup

Beautiful Soup, so rich and green,
Waiting in a hot tureen!
Who for such dainties would not stoop?
Soup of the evening, beautiful Soup!
Soup of the evening, beautiful Soup!
   Beau—ootiful Soo—oop!
   Beau—ootiful Soo—oop!
Soo—oop of the e—e—evening,
   Beautiful, beautiful Soup!

Beautiful Soup! Who cares for fish,
Game, or any other dish?
Who would not give all else for two p—*
   ennyworth only of beautiful Soup?
Pennyworth only of beautiful Soup?
   Beau—ootiful Soo—oop!
   Beau—ootiful Soo—oop!
Soo—oop of the e—e—evening,
   Beau—ti—ful, beauti—FUL SOUP!

*pronounced "toop"
            Lewis Carroll

Try reading the poem together. Let one person read the first five lines of each verse, then everyone join in on the chorus. Which line is the most fun to read?

The Centipede's Song is from a book called *James and the Giant Peach* by Roald Dahl.

The Centipede's Song

'I've eaten many strange and scrumptious dishes
   in my time,
Like jellied gnats and dandyprats and earwigs
   cooked in slime,
And mice with rice — they're really nice
When roasted in their prime.
(But don't forget to sprinkle them with just a pinch
   of grime.)

'I've eaten fresh mudburgers by the greatest cooks
   there are,
And scrambled dregs and stinkbug's eggs and
   hornets stewed in tar,
And pails of snails and lizards' tails,
And beetles by the jar.
(A beetle is improved by just a splash of vinegar.)

'I often eat boiled slobbages. They're grand when
   served beside
Minced doodlebugs and curried slugs. And have you
   ever tried
Mosquitoes' toes and wampfish roes
Most delicately fried?
(The only trouble is they disagree with my inside.)

'I'm mad for crispy wasp-stings on a piece of
    buttered toast,
And pickled spines of porcupines. And then a
    gorgeous roast
Of dragon's flesh, well hung, not fresh—
It costs a pound at most,
(And comes to you in barrels if you order it by post.)

'I crave the tasty tentacles of octopi for tea.
I like hot-dogs, I LOVE hot-frogs, and surely
    you'll agree
A plate of soil with engine oil's
A super recipe.
(I hardly need to mention that it's practically free.)

'For dinner on my birthday shall I tell you what I chose?
Hot noodles made from poodles on a slice of
    garden hose—
And a rather smelly jelly
Made of armadillo's toes.
(The jelly is delicious, but you have to hold your nose.')

Roald Dahl

Which do you think is the most horrible food
the centipede mentions?

ACTIVITY: **A Food Collage**

*"For dinner on my birthday shall I tell you
what I chose: Hot noodles made from poodles
on a slice of garden hose."*

What would *you* choose for dinner on your
birthday? Think of the foods you like best.
Make a collage picture to show your birthday
meal.

1. Cut a large circle out of white paper. This is
   your birthday dinner plate. (You could use a
   real paper plate if you have one.)
2. Now make the food. You can cut pictures
   out of magazines, draw them yourself or
   make "model food" (e.g. screwed-up orange
   paper lumps for baked beans).
3. Stick your birthday food on to your plate to
   make a collage.

UNIT FOUR

R. L. S.

Robert Louis Stevenson was born in Edinburgh, Scotland, in 1850. His father was a lighthouse builder and quite rich. Robert Louis was not a strong child and he had to stay in bed a lot when he was young. His mother and his nurse used to keep him happy by reading stories and poems to him. Robert Louis grew to love books of all kinds and when he was older he became a famous writer of stories for adults. He became known all over the world as R. L. S. – one of the few people in history who are often known just by their initials.

But R. L. S. never forgot what it was like to be a child, and he wrote many poems for children. These poems are still popular today, even though R. L. S. died in 1894. Most of his best poems are grouped together in a book called *A Child's Garden of Verses*. Here are a few of them:

A Good Play

We built a ship upon the stairs
All made of the back-bedroom chairs,
And filled it full of sofa pillows
To go a-sailing on the billows.

We took a saw and several nails,
And water in the nursery pails;
And Tom said, "Let us also take
An apple and a slice of cake;" —
Which was enough for Tom and me
To go a-sailing on, till tea.

We sailed along for days and days,
And had the very best of plays;
But Tom fell out and hurt his knee,
So there was no one left but me.

Robert Louis Stevenson

Have you ever made up a game using ordinary household things?
What was it and what did you do?

Escape at Bedtime

The lights from the parlour and kitchen shone out
Through the blinds and the windows and bars;
And high overhead and all moving about,
There were thousands of millions of stars.
There ne'er were such thousands of leaves on a tree,
Nor of people in church or the park,
As the crowds of the stars that looked down upon me,
And that glittered and winked in the dark.
The Dog, and the Plough, and the Hunter, and all,
And the star of the sailor, and Mars,
These shone in the sky, and the pail by the wall
Would be half full of water and stars.
They saw me at last, and they chased me with cries,
And they soon had me packed into bed;
But the glory kept shining and bright in my eyes,
And the stars going round in my head.

Robert Louis Stevenson

The Pole Star
(the star of the sailor, because
it guides him to the North)

The Constellation
of Orion
(The Hunter)

Orion's Belt

The Constellation
of the Plough

Sirius, the Dog Star

Orion and Sirius
are seen in Britain
only in the winter.

Who are "they", who chased the child to bed?
Do you know any of the stars mentioned in the
poem? (Look at the picture of the star
constellations opposite. It will help you
to find the stars in the sky at night.)

Windy Nights

Whenever the moon and stars are set,
 Whenever the wind is high,
All night long in the dark and wet,
 A man goes riding by.
Late in the night when the fires are out,
Why does he gallop
 and gallop about?

Whenever the trees are crying aloud,
 And ships are tossed at sea,
By, on the highway, low and loud,
 By at the gallop goes he.
By at the gallop he goes, and then
By he comes back at the gallop again.

Robert Louis Stevenson

The speaker in the poem only hears the
horseman on certain sorts of nights. What kind
of nights? Who do you think the speaker is?
Does a horseman really go riding by?

ACTIVITY: **Wax Resist Silhouette**

Make a *Windy Nights* picture.

1. Draw a picture of a horse and rider on white paper. (If you find this very hard you could use the picture in the book to help you.) Colour your horse and rider black using wax crayons. Put a good thick layer of black wax on to the paper.

2. Cut your horseman picture out and stick it on to a big sheet of white paper.

3. Use other dark-coloured wax crayons to draw the other things mentioned in the poem around your horseman.

4. Make some very watery grey paint. Paint over your whole picture with this. The paint will not stick to the wax and so all the things you crayoned will stand out clearly against the grey background.

5. As an extra touch, you might like to add the moon and the stars in silver foil.

N.B. Mars is a planet, not a star. It shines at night with the sun's reflected light, and has a reddish glow.

My Shadow

I have a little shadow that goes in and out with me,
And what can be the use of him is more than I can
    see,
He is very, very like me from the heels up to the
    head;
And I see him jump before me, when I jump into
    my bed.

The funniest thing about him is the way he likes to
    grow –
Not at all like proper children, which is always very
    slow;
For he sometimes shoots up taller like an india-
    rubber ball,
And he sometimes gets so little that there's none of
    him at all.

He hasn't got a notion of how children ought to play,
And can only make a fool of me in every sort of way.
He stays so close beside me, he's a coward you can
    see;
I'd think shame to stick to nursie as that shadow
    sticks to me!

One morning, very early, before the sun was up,
I rose and found the shining dew on every
    buttercup;
But my lazy little shadow, like an arrant sleepy-
    head,
Had stayed at home behind me and was fast asleep
    in bed.

Robert Louis Stevenson

When do you think you'd usually have no shadow?
And when is your shadow usually longest?

20

In the 19th century, town streets were lit by gas-lamps. Lamplighters were employed to light them each evening. There was a gas-lamp in the street outside R.L.S.'s front door.

The Lamplighter

My tea is nearly ready
   and the sun has left the sky;
It's time to take the window
   to see Leerie going by;
For every night at tea-time
   and before you take your seat,
With lantern and with ladder
   he comes posting up the street.

Now Tom would be a driver
   and Maria go to sea,
And my papa's a banker
   and as rich as he can be;
But I, when I am stronger
   and can choose what I'm to do,
O Leerie, I'll go round at night
   and light the lamps with you!

For we are very lucky,
   with a lamp before the door,
And Leerie stops to light it
   as he lights so many more;
And O! before you hurry by
   with ladder and with light,
O Leerie, see a little child
   and nod to him to-night!

Robert Louis Stevenson

Do you ever watch out for someone like Leerie in your street?

Colours

from **What is Red?**

Red is a sunset
Blazing and bright
Red is feeling brave
With all your might.
Red is a sunburn
Spot on your nose,
Sometimes red
Is a red, red rose.

Red squiggles out
When you cut your hand.
Red is a brick and
The sound of a band.
Red is a hotness
You get inside
When you're embarrassed
And want to hide.

The poet lists a lot of things that are red. How many can you remember without looking back at the poem?
Check to see how many you missed.
Most of the things in the poem are red to look at. But the poet also talks about two things that she thinks *sound* red. Try to find them.
Do you agree that these things *sound* red?
What else *sounds* red to you?
She also puts in the poem some things that you can't see or hear at all. She thinks they *feel* red. Try to find them all.
What else has a red feeling to it?
What do you think *smells* red?

Fire-cracker, fire-engine
Fire-flicker red—
And when you're angry
Red runs through your head.
Red is a lipstick,
Red is a shout,
Red is a signal
That says: 'Watch out!'

Red is a great big
Rubber ball.
Red is the giant-est
Colour of all.
Red is a show-off
No doubt about it—
But can you imagine
Living without it?

Mary O'Neill

22

What is Grey?

Grey is the colour of an elephant
And a mouse
And a tumbledown house.
It's fog and smog,
And very fine print,
It's a hush and
The wetness of melting slush.
Tiredness and oysters
Both are grey,
Smoke swirls
And grandmother's curls.
So are some spring coats
And nanny-goats.
Pigeons are grey
And a rainy day
The sad look of a slum
And chewing gum.
Pussy willows are grey
In a velvety way.
Suits, shoes
And bad news,
Beggars' hats
And alley cats
Skin of a mole
And a worn slipper sole.
Content is grey
And sleepiness, too.
They wear grey suede gloves
When they're touching you . . .

Mary O'Neill

Some of the grey things in this poem are nice and some are nasty.
Which are the nice grey things? Which are the nasty ones?
What else does the colour grey remind you of, besides the things Mary O'Neill has listed?
What *sounds* grey? What *feels* grey?
What *smells* grey?

ACTIVITY: **Writing Colour Poems**

1. Try writing a class poem about another colour with your teacher. Your teacher can write your ideas on the board as you think of them. Your poem does not have to rhyme, but you should start each new thought on a new line.
2. Try another colour poem on your own. Choose a colour and think of as many things as you can that it reminds you of. Think of things that *look, sound, feel* and *smell* that colour.
   Don't try to make your poem rhyme, but remember to start each new thought on a new line. And start each new line with a capital letter like the poems in this unit.

UNIT SIX

Obbly Gubbly

The two poems in this unit use the *sounds* of words to get their effect. The poets have chosen words that *sound like* what they are describing. Sometimes they have even invented new words.

Both poems, particularly the second one, are quite difficult to read out loud. You have to read them a few times to get the feel of the words and the rhythm.

Sink Song

Scouring out the porridge pot,
   Round and round and round!

Out with all the scraith and scoopery.
Lift the eely ooly droopery,
Chase the glubbery slubbery gloopery
   Round and round and round!

Out with all the doleful dithery,
Ladle out the slimery slithery,
Hunt and catch the hithery thithery,
   Round and round and round!

Out with all the obbly gubbly,
On the stove it burns so bubbly,
Use the spoon and use it doubly,
   Round and round and round!

J. A. Lindon

Weather

Dot a dot dot dot a dot dot
Spotting the window pane.

Spack a spack speck flick a flack fleck
Freckling the window pane.

A spatter a scatter a wet cat a clatter
A splatter a rumble outside.

Umbrella umbrella umbrella umbrella
Bumbershoot barrel of rain.

Slosh a galosh slosh a galosh
Slither and slather a glide.

A puddle a jump a puddle a jump
A puddle a jump puddle splosh.

A juddle a pump a luddle a dump
A pudmuddle jump in and slide!

Eve Merriam

Many of these words and groups of words have wonderful sounds. It is great fun to say them, to roll them around your mouth. Which lines do you like best? Why?

ACTIVITY: **Making Sounds**

Work in pairs.
Choose one of the poems and make up some sounds to go with the words. You could use:
1) percussion instruments – drums, chime bars, triangle;
2) your voices (*not* loudly);
3) anything around you. You could tap a ruler on a desk, scratch a pencil against paper, and so on.

Work it out so that one of you can read the poem while the other person makes the sounds that go with it.
When your teacher calls you together, some pairs can perform their poems and sounds. Perhaps you could even tape some.

Which Witch . . .?

This poem about a witch was written more than three hundred years ago:

The Hag

The Hag is astride,
    This night for to ride;
The Devil and she together:
    Through thick, and through thin,
    Now out, and then in,   5
Though ne'er so foul be the weather.

A Thorn or a Burr
    She takes for a Spur:
With a lash of a Bramble she rides now,
    Through Brakes and through Briars,   10
    O'er Ditches, and Mires,
She follows the Spirit that guides now.

No Beast, for his food,
    Dares now range the wood;
But hush't in his lair he lies lurking;   15
    While mischiefs, by these,
    On Land and on Seas,
At noon of Night are a-working.

The storm will arise,
    And trouble the skies;   20
This night, and more for the wonder,
    The ghost from the Tomb
    Affrighted shall come,
Called out by the clap of the Thunder.

Robert Herrick

What do these words mean:

astride (line 1)   *foul* (line 6)
spur (line 8)   *mires*? (line 11)

What do you think the poet means by *At noon of Night*? Listen to your teacher read the poem again. Follow in your book.
Which do you think is the spookiest line?

Here is a modern poem about a witch who isn't very good at her job:

Mixed Brews

There once was a witch
Who lived in a ditch
And brewed her brews in the hedges,
She gathered some dank
From the deepest bank
And some from around the edges.

She practised her charms
By waving her arms
And muttering words and curses;
And every spell
Would have worked out well
If she hadn't mixed the verses.

Not long since,
When she wanted a Prince
To wake the Sleeping Beauty,
A man appeared
With a long grey beard,
Too old to report for duty!

When she hoped to save
Aladdin's cave
From his uncle cruel and cranky,
She concocted a spell
That somehow fell
Not on him but on Widow Twankey.

With a magic bean
She called for a Quee
Who was locked in the wizard's castle.
There came an old hag
With a postman's bag
And threepence to pay on the parcel.

What *comes* of a witch
Who has hitch after hitch?
I'm afraid that there's no telling:
But I think as a rule.
She returns to school
And tries to improve her spelling.

Clive Sansom

What do you think the poet means by the last line?
Try tapping out the rhythm of the first verse of *The Hag* as your teacher reads it out loud.
Then try tapping out the rhythm of the first verse of *Mixed Brews*.
What do you notice?

27

The last poem is by an American poet who never used capital letters. He even signed his own name without capital letters. His poem may not make sense to you at first. Try reading it a few times, and listening to the *sounds* of the words he uses. Also notice the way he *spaces* his words. The spaces tell you where to pause for a moment.

Hist Whist

hist   whist
little ghostthings
tip-toe
twinkle-toe

little twitchy
witches and tingling
goblins
hob-a-nob   hob-a-nob

little hoppy happy
toad in tweeds
tweeds
little itchy mousies

with scuttling
eyes   rustle and run   and
hidehidehide
whisk

whisk   look out for the old woman
with the wart on her nose
what she'll do to yer
nobody knows

for she knows the devil   ooch
the devil   ouch
the devil
ach   the great

green
dancing
devil
devil

devil
devil
  wheeEEE

e. e. cummings

Which witch poem do you like best? Why?

ACTIVITY 1: **Voices and Sounds**

You are going to make a voice and sound presentation of *Hist Whist*.

1. Work in groups of about four. Each group should work on one small part of the poem (perhaps four lines). You may want the whole class to join in for the end.
2. In your group, decide how you are going to say the words. Who is going to say what? How fast or slow are you going to say each bit? When are you going to pause? When will your voice be high and when will it be low? When will it be soft and when will it be loud?
3. Make up some sound effects to go with your part of the poem.
4. When everyone is ready, put the whole thing together. It might be fun to make a tape-recording if you can.

ACTIVITY 2: **Making a Witch**

1. Make a narrow cone of thick black paper or card.

2. Make a circle of the same paper or card. Cut another circle in the middle, so it will slide on to the top of the cone to make a witch's hat.

3. Make a witch face on an oval of white paper and stick it on the cone under the hat.

4. Add stringy hair around the face (wool or strips of paper).

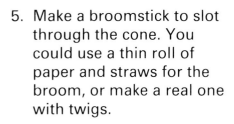

5. Make a broomstick to slot through the cone. You could use a thin roll of paper and straws for the broom, or make a real one with twigs.

6. Finish off the witch's cloak by sticking on silver and gold stars.

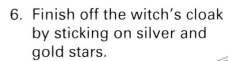

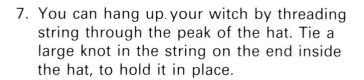

7. You can hang up your witch by threading string through the peak of the hat. Tie a large knot in the string on the end inside the hat, to hold it in place.

Hands Together, Eyes Closed

Some people say prayers to God every night before they go to sleep. Here are two prayers which people in Britain have been saying for hundreds of years. They both ask God for protection and safety at night.

Matthew, Mark, Luke and John,
Bless the bed that I lie on;
Four corners to my bed,
Four angels there be spread:
One at my head, one at my feet,
And two to guard me while I sleep.
God within and God without,
And Jesus Christ all round about;
I go by sea, I go by land,
The Lord made me with His right hand.
If any danger come to me,
Sweet Jesus Christ deliver me.
He's the branch and I'm the flower,
Pray God send me a happy hour.
And if I die before I wake,
I pray the Lord my soul to take.

From ghoulies and ghosties
And long-leggetty beasties,
And things that go bump in the night,
Good Lord, deliver us.

Both these prayers are from the Christian religion. Perhaps you know some from other religions.
Do you ever say prayers? If so, what prayers do you know?

The next two poems are meant to be prayers from animals to God.

Prayer of the Ox

Dear God, give me time.
Men are always so driven!
Make them understand that I can never hurry.
Give me time to eat.
Give me time to plod.
Give me time to sleep.
Give me time to think.
Amen.

translated by Rumer Godden

Prayer of the Little Ducks

Dear God,
give us a flood of water.
Let it rain tomorrow and always.
Give us plenty of little slugs
and other luscious things to eat.
Protect all folk who quack
and everyone who knows how to swim.
Amen.

translated by Rumer Godden

ACTIVITY: Poetry Writing

The two prayers ask God for things that the Ox and the Little Ducks want and need. What do you think a cat would ask for? What would a dog ask for? What about a hamster or a gerbil? Choose an animal and write a prayer from your animal to God. Here are some hints:

1. Write your prayer as a poem. Look at *Prayer of the Ox* and *Prayer of the Little Ducks* to help you.
2. Your poem does not have to rhyme.
3. Remember to keep your lines short, and to start each line with a capital letter.

Jaws!

The Shark

A treacherous monster is the Shark
He never makes the least remark.

And when he sees you on the sand,
He doesn't seem to want to land.

He watches you take off your clothes, 5
And not the least excitement shows.

His eyes do not grow bright or roll,
He has astounding self-control.

He waits till you are quite undrest,
And seems to take no interest. 10

And when towards the sea you leap,
He looks as if he were asleep.

But when you once get in his range,
His whole demeanour seems to change.

He throws his body right about, 15
And his true character comes out.

It's no use crying or appealing,
He seems to lose all decent feeling.

After this warning you will wish
To keep clear of this treacherous fish. 20

His back is black, his stomach white,
He has a very dangerous bite.

Lord Alfred Douglas

What do these words mean: *treacherous* (line 1), *demeanour* (line 14)?
What do you know about sharks?
Read the poem again – let eleven people take two lines each.
Do you agree that the shark is a *treacherous monster*?

The Teeth of Sharks

The thing about a shark is—teeth,
One row above, one row beneath.

Now take a close look. Do you find
It has another row behind?

Still closer—here, I'll hold your hat:
Has it a third row behind that?

Now look in and . . . Look out! Oh my,
I'll *never* know now! Well, goodbye.

John Ciardi

What happens at the end of this poem?
Why do you think the shark has several rows of teeth?

The next poem is about a *chivalrous* or well-mannered shark. There may be some words in it that you don't understand at first, but don't worry. Listen to your teacher reading it, and follow in your book. What matters is that you understand what is happening in the poem.

The Rhyme of the Chivalrous Shark

Most chivalrous fish of the ocean,
To ladies forbearing and mild,
Though his record be dark is the man-eating shark
Who will eat neither woman nor child.

He dines upon seamen and skippers,
And tourists his hunger assuage,
And a fresh cabin boy will inspire him with joy
If he's past the maturity age.

A doctor, a lawyer, a preacher,
He'll gobble one any fine day,
But the ladies, God bless 'em, he'll only address 'em
Politely and go on his way.

I can readily cite you an instance
Where a lovely young lady of Breem,
Who was tender and sweet and delicious to eat,
Fell into the bay with a scream.

She struggled and flounced in the water
And signalled in vain for her bark,
And she'd surely been drowned if she hadn't been found
By a chivalrous man-eating shark.

He bowed in a manner most polished,
Thus soothing her impulses wild;
"Don't be frightened," he said, "I've been properly bred
And will eat neither woman nor child."

Then he proferred his fin and she took it—
Such a gallantry none can dispute—
While the passengers cheered as the vessel they neared
And a broadside was fired in salute.

And they soon stood alongside the vessel,
When a life-saving dinghy was lowered
With the pick of the crew, and her relatives too,
And the mate and the skipper aboard.

So they took her aboard in a jiffy,
Shark stood to attention the while,
Then he rose on his flipper and ate up the skipper
And went on his way with a smile.

And this shows the prince of the ocean
To ladies forbearing and mild,
Though his record be dark is the man-eating shark
Who will eat neither woman nor child.

Wallace Irving

The shark in the poem is a *man-eating* shark. What does this usually mean? What does it mean in the poem?

ACTIVITY 1: **Dramatisation**

Try acting out the story of the *Chivalrous Shark*.

1. Choose a good reader, or your teacher, to be the narrator. The narrator is the person who will read the poem aloud. The only bits of the poem the narrator will not read are the words spoken by the shark.
2. Choose someone to be the lady, someone to be the shark, someone to be the mate, and someone to be the skipper.
3. Divide everyone else into two groups, one group bigger than the other. The people in the big group are to be the passengers. The people in the smaller group are to be the lady's relatives.
4. Start off with the shark swimming about in the water while the narrator reads the first three verses. Then act out the rest of the story.

ACTIVITY 2: **Shark Mobile**

1. Cut two shark body shapes (exactly the same) from black paper, and put them one on top of the other.
2. Glue the fins and tails together.

3. Staple around the edges of the rest of the body, leaving a gap at the belly.
4. Use this gap to stuff the shark with crumpled newspaper. Staple up the gap.
5. Glue white paper on both sides for the white belly.
6. Glue silver foil teeth on both sides of the mouth and give the shark two evil eyes.
7. Hang the mobile by a string from the fin. If it doesn't balance properly, push the paper about inside the body until it does.

Rolls Royce, Fiat, Ford

The Traffic Light

HALT! My eye is red!
Rolls-Royce, Fiat, Ford,
Halt there, I said.
Down the obedient road,
Brute engines muted,
The meek traffic stands in line
Awaiting my eye of green.

For I command them all!
By day and quiet night
Aloof I stand, and tall,
Banded in black and white.
I am all-powerful.
With one flick of my eye,
It is I who will let them by.

But first, a touch of amber.
A cautious warning.
Now hear the engines roar,
The gears groaning.
Green! Like a stream they pour
Into the city's maze,
On their mysterious ways.

I stand on my one toe
Unable to turn my head
Oh, how I'd love to know,
As past they speed,
Where they all go.
HALT. My eye is red!
Halt there, I said.

But quite soon I'll let you go.

Leslie Norris

How powerful is the traffic light? What things can it do and what things can't it do? Are the cars in the poem powerful or not?

We are used to cars, but what might they look like to someone who had never seen one before?

Car Fodder

There is a strange man in the city
Trying to feed the cars.
He says he has come on holiday
From his home on planet Mars.

He says he is very worried
Because the cars won't eat
And that he knows they must be hungry
Because all they do is bleat.

Brian Patten

The Martian thinks the cars are animals. In what ways do they seem like animals to him? In what other ways can cars seem like animals?

Carbreakers

There's a graveyard in our street,
But it's not for putting people in;
The bodies that they bury here
Are made of steel and paint and tin.

The people come and leave their wrecks
For crunching in the giant jaws
Of a great hungry car-machine,
That lives on bonnets, wheels and doors.

When I pass by the yard at night,
I sometimes think I hear a sound
Of ghostly horns that moan and whine,
Upon that metal-graveyard mound.

Marion Lines

This is a good poem for reading with sound-effects. Let some people read out the poem while others make the noises mentioned in the background.

ACTIVITY: A Traffic Survey

During the day a stream of traffic will be passing by somewhere near your school. It can be very good fun to go out and watch this traffic. If you watch carefully you can often spot some interesting facts and patterns about your local traffic.

1. Decide what you are going to look for. Here are some suggestions: types of vehicle; direction of traffic; makes of car; colours of cars.

2. Work in pairs. Each pair should be in charge of a topic. Several pairs can work on the same topic. It is interesting to see if their results are similar.

3. Work out a survey sheet for you and your partner to use, e.g.

Types of Vehicle Passing on North Street at 10 a.m.

cars
vans
buses
lorries
motorbikes
pushbikes

4. Practise tallying, e.g.

III   stands for 3
IIII   stands for 5
IIII IIII stands for 10, etc.

5. Go out and do your survey. Work for about ten minutes.

6. When you come back write down what you found out, e.g. "Mary and I found out that 12 cars, 1 van, 4 lorries, 2 buses, and no motorbikes or pushbikes passed by."

7. Can you use this information to make a sensible guess about any patterns in your local traffic? e.g. "Mary and I think that cars are popular on North Street but bikes are not."

8. Your teacher may help you to draw some graphs of your findings.

9. Try to make a class Traffic Survey display.

Big and Little, Great and Small

There is a very famous story called *Gulliver's Travels*, by Jonathan Swift. In this story Gulliver goes to a land called Lilliput. The people in this land are very small and to them Gulliver seems like a huge giant.

Gulliver in Lilliput

From his nose
Clouds he blows.
When he speaks,
Thunder breaks.
When he eats,
Famine threats.
When he treads,
Mountains' heads
Groan and shake;
Armies quake.
See him stride
Valleys wide,
Over woods,
Over floods.
Troops take heed,
Man and steed:
Left and right,
Speed your flight!
In amaze
Lost I gaze
Toward the skies:
See! and believe your eyes!

Alexander Pope

Imagine that you could grow into a giant and stand in your school playground. What might happen?

The next poem reminds us that in some ways we *are* giants. The name in the first line is pronounced *Lurv – en – hock*.

The Microscope

Anton Leeuwenhoek was Dutch.
He sold pincushions, cloth, and such.
The waiting townsfolk fumed and fussed
As Anton's dry goods gathered dust.

He worked, instead of tending store,
At grinding special lenses for
A microscope. Some of the things
He looked at were:

       mosquitoes' wings,
the hairs of sheep, the legs of lice,
the skin of people, dogs, and mice;
ox eyes, spiders' spinning gear,
fishes' scales, a little smear
of his own blood,

      and best of all,
the unknown, busy, very small
bugs that swim and bump and hop
inside a simple water drop.

Impossible! Most Dutchmen said.
This Anton's crazy in the head.
We ought to ship him off to Spain.
He says he's seen a housefly's brain.

He says the water that we drink
Is full of bugs. He's mad, we think!

They called him *dumkopf*, which means dope.
That's how we got the microscope.

Maxine Kumin

Have you ever used a microscope or any other piece of equipment which makes small things look bigger? If so, what did you see?

ACTIVITY: A Matchbox Collection

Miniature, or small things, can be very attractive. They are often great fun to collect. What sort of collections of small things do people sometimes make?
There is one sort of collection of small things which is very quick and easy to make. All you need is a matchbox, and all you have to do is fit as many different tiny objects into it as possible. (You can only have one of each sort of thing.) Perhaps your teacher would let you have a class competition – the person with the most objects in the matchbox wins.

The Train to Glasgow

All the poems in this unit are by a poet called Wilma Horsbrugh (born 1903). A lot of Wilma Horsbrugh's poetry is written in the form of a rhyming story which repeats itself. The verses tend to get longer and longer. Her poems were popular on radio for many years, and indeed the last edition of her poetry was published by the BBC (*The Bold Bad Bus and Other Rhyming Stories*, BBC 1973).

The Train to Glasgow

Sometimes it can be good fun to vary the *rhythm* with this kind of poetry. You can accelerate it in places, by reading faster and faster. Or you can d-e-c-e-l-e-r-a-t-e it and slow the reading down and down (and perhaps make your voice get deeper and deeper). Try varying the rhythm a little in order to make an amusing reading of this poem.

Here is the train to Glasgow.
Here is the driver,
Mr MacIver,
Who drove the train to Glasgow.
Here is the guard from Donibristle
Who waved his flag and blew his whistle
To tell the driver,
Mr MacIver,
To start the train to Glasgow.

Here is a boy called Donald MacBrain
Who came to the station to catch the train
But saw the guard from Donibristle
Wave his flag and blow his whistle
To tell the driver,
Mr MacIver,
To start the train to Glasgow.

Here is the guard, a kindly man
Who, at the last moment, hauled into the van
That fortunate boy called Donald MacBrain
Who came to the station to catch the train
But saw the guard from Donibristle
Wave his flag and blow his whistle
To tell the driver,
Mr MacIver,
To start the train to Glasgow.

Here are hens and here are cocks,
Clucking and crowing inside a box,
In charge of the guard, that kindly man
Who, at the last moment, hauled into the van
That fortunate boy called Donald MacBrain
Who came to the station to catch the train
But saw the guard from Donibristle
Wave his flag and blow his whistle
To tell the driver,
Mr MacIver,
To start the train to Glasgow.

41

Here is the train. It gave a jolt
Which loosened a catch and loosened a bolt,
And let out the hens and let out the cocks,
Clucking and crowing out of their box,
In charge of the guard, that kindly man
Who, at the last moment, hauled into the van
That fortunate boy called Donald MacBrain
Who came to the station to catch the train
But saw the guard from Donibristle
Wave his flag and blow his whistle
To tell the driver,
Mr MacIver,
To start the train to Glasgow.

The guard chased a hen and, missing it, fell.
The hens were all squawking, the cocks were as well.
And unless you were there you haven't a notion
Of the flurry, the fuss, the noise and commotion
Caused by the train which gave a jolt
And loosened a catch and loosened a bolt
And let out the hens and let out the cocks,
Clucking and crowing out of their box,
In charge of the guard, that kindly man
Who, at the last moment, hauled into the van
That fortunate boy called Donald MacBrain
Who came to the station to catch the train
But saw the guard from Donibristle
Wave his flag and blow his whistle
To tell the driver,
Mr MacIver,
To start the train to Glasgow.

Now Donald was quick and Donald was neat
And Donald was nimble on his feet.
He caught the hens and he caught the cocks
And he put them back in their big box.
The guard was pleased as pleased could be
And invited Donald to come to tea
On Saturday, at Donibristle,
And let him blow his lovely whistle
And said in all his life he'd never
Seen a boy so quick and clever,
And so did the driver,
Mr MacIver
Who drove the train to Glasgow.

Wilma Horsbrugh

The Cake

This poem can be nicely dramatised, or read around the class. There should be different readers for the farmer, the miller, the woman, the cow Nell, the hen, and the cake. Someone will also need to read the bits about the oven, and the table set for tea.

You can read many of Wilma Horsbrugh's poems in this way.

I am the farmer, I live at Strathblane,
I plough my fields and sow my grain.

I am the miller at Campsie Glen.
I ground the corn that was cut by the men
Employed by the farmer who lived at Strathblane,
Who ploughed his fields and sowed his grain.

I am the woman who kneaded the dough,
Made from the flour as white as snow,
Bought from the miller at Campsie Glen,
Who ground the corn that was cut by the men
Employed by the farmer who lived at Strathblane,
Who ploughed his fields and sowed his grain.

Here is the milk and butter as well
That came from a cow whose name was Nell,
Owned by the woman who kneaded the dough,
Made from the flour as white as snow,
Bought from the miller at Campsie Glen,
Who ground the corn that was cut by the men
Employed by the farmer who lived at Strathblane,
Who ploughed his fields and sowed his grain.

Here is the oven in which the cake
Was placed for an hour and more to bake,
Watched by the hen with yellow legs,
Who provided the handsome new-laid eggs
To mix with the milk and butter as well,
That came from the cow whose name was Nell,
Owned by the woman who kneaded the dough,
Made from the flour as white as snow,
Bought from the miller at Campsie Glen,
Who ground the corn that was cut by the men
Employed by the farmer who lived at Strathblane,
Who ploughed his fields and sowed his grain.

Here is the cake – without a doubt
Done to a turn – now lifted out
Of the nice hot oven in which the cake
Was placed for an hour and more to bake,
Watched by the hen with yellow legs,
Who provided the handsome new-laid eggs
To mix with the milk and butter as well,
That came from the cow whose name was Nell,
Owned by the woman who kneaded the dough,
Made from the flour as white as snow,
Bought from the miller at Campsie Glen,
Who ground the corn that was cut by the men
Employed by the farmer who lived at Strathblane,
Who ploughed his fields and sowed his grain.

Here is the table set for tea,
With cups and plates for you and me,
And the beautiful cake – without a doubt
Done to a turn – now lifted out
Of the nice hot oven in which the cake
Was placed for an hour and more to bake,
Watched by the hen with yellow legs,
Who provided the handsome new-laid eggs
To mix with the milk and butter as well
That came from the cow whose name was Nell,
Owned by the woman who kneaded the dough,
Made from the flour as white as snow,
Bought from the miller at Campsie Glen,
Who ground the corn that was cut by the men
Employed by the farmer of Strathblane,
Who ploughed his fields and sowed his grain.

Wilma Horsbrugh

Here is the hen with the yellow legs,
Who provided the handsome new-laid eggs,
To mix with the milk and butter as well,
That came from the cow whose name was Nell,
Owned by the woman who kneaded the dough,
Made from the flour as white as snow,
Bought from the miller at Campsie Glen,
Who ground the corn that was cut by the men
Employed by the farmer who lived at Strathblane,
Who ploughed his fields and sowed his grain.

The Cobbler's Shop

Some folk walk with a skip and a trip
And others go "Clop-clop"
But all the feet going down our street
Have shoes from the cobbler's shop.
With a rap tap tap and a tip tap top,
The cobbler mends our shoes
And the children stop at the cobbler's shop
To see what tools he'll use.
With a rap tap tap and a tip tap top,
Tip tap, tip tap, cobbler's shop!

My mother's shoes are shiny black,
She hurries out and she hurries back.

My father's shoes are big and brown,
He wears them when he goes to town.

Baby's shoes are wee and red,
He tries to put them on in bed!

The coalman's shoes have great thick soles,
They go *"Clump-clump!"* as he carries coals.

Auntie Sue has tremendous heels,
She's off to the shop for cotton reels.

The policeman's shoes are rubbery stuff,
I hope they keep him warm enough.

And *I* have nice new shoes that squeak,
I've walked *"Squeak-squawk!"* for nearly a week!

Feet in sandals, feet in shoes
Of brilliant colours, reds and blues,
Boots with tackets, boots without,
They clatter, stump or stroll about,
And some folk walk with a skip and a trip
And others go "Clop-clop!"
But all the feet going down our street
Have shoes from the cobbler's shop
With a rap tap tap and a tip tap top,
The cobbler mends our shoes,
And the children stop at the cobbler's shop,
To see what tools he'll use.
With a rap tap tap and a tip tap top,
Tip tap, tip tap, cobbler's shop.

Wilma Horsbrugh

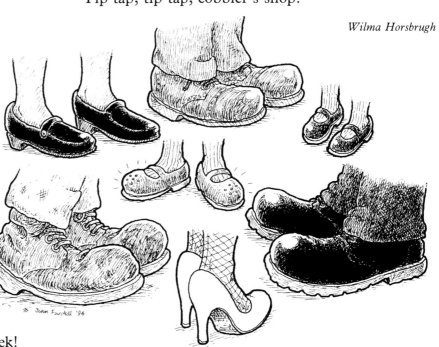

Night-bears

This is a good-night poem for younger children.
Could you recite it softly? Try to get the children in
the mood for going to sleep.

Three little bears
From nowhere in particular,
   nowhere in particular,
   nowhere at all,
Came up the stairs
And climbed the perpendicular
   climbed the perpendicular,
   nursery wall.

They sat upon the ceiling
And sang with all their might
Songs so full of feeling
They lasted half the night.

A funny thing it seemed
For little bears to do.
I think I must have dreamed
Those little bears, don't you?

For when the songs were ended
Then down the wall they slid,
And when they had descended
Do you know what they did?

Those three little bears
Went nowhere in particular,
   nowhere in particular,
   flat or perpendicular,
   nowhere at all.

ACTIVITY: **Make a frieze**
Make a wall picture or frieze of the poem *The
Cake* or *The Train to Glasgow*. Everybody will need
to do one part of the picture. Try to get all the bits
of the poem into the picture.

46

Wilma Horsbrugh

Biographical Notes on Poets

LEWIS CARROLL (1832 – 1898)
Real name Charles Dodgson. A shy retiring man who taught maths at Christ Church College, Oxford. Fond of children. Wrote *Alice's Adventures In Wonderland* to amuse Alice Liddell, daughter of the Dean of Christ Church.

ROALD DAHL (1916 – 1992)
Born in Wales. Name Norwegian in origin. Fought as fighter pilot in Middle East 1940–1941. Married to actress Patricia Neal. Author of many popular children's books. Sophie, the heroine of *The B.F.G.*, one of his books, is based on one of his grand-daughters and looks just like her.

Roald Dahl

WILMA HORSBRUGH (1903 –   )
Born at Blanefield in Stirlingshire, not far from "the farmer who lived at Strathblane" (about whom you can read in her poem *The Cake*). In the 1930s, she started to contribute poems for broadcasting by "Aunt Kathleen" (or Kathleen Garscadden) on the pioneering BBC Scotland Children's Hour. She also recalls reading her "building rhymes" to entertain young children who were long-stay TB patients in hospital at Bannockburn. The children loved to join in these recitations with her. Mrs Horsbrugh's poetry has also proved popular in Europe – children learning English enjoy its regular repetitions. Mrs Horsbrugh now lives in a very beautiful part of Perthshire, at the village of Killin near the head of Loch Tay.

EVE MERRIAM
Born in Philadelphia, U.S.A. Says, "I always wrote – even when I was young." Now writes poetry for children and adults. Is married to another writer and has two grown-up sons. Lives in New York.

BRIAN PATTEN (7th Feb. 1946 –   )
Writes children's books and poetry. Also writes plays for theatre and television. His poetry has been translated into Dutch, German, Italian, Polish and Spanish.

ALEXANDER POPE (1688–1744)
Son of a linen-draper. Always very clever for his age. Didn't go to school. Instead stayed at home and read and wrote poetry. At 12 developed a disease of the spine and never grew above 5 feet tall. Had to wear a steel frame all his life to keep himself upright. Rather a sharp-natured man, perhaps as a result of all the pain and teasing he suffered.

LORD ALFRED DOUGLAS (22nd Oct. 1870 – 1945)
Son of Marquis of Queensberry (Queensberry Rules in boxing). Fine steeplechase runner at school. Noted for his good looks and charm. A close friend of the poet, Oscar Wilde. Once sent to prison for publishing a rude comment about Winston Churchill.

ELEANOR FARJEON (1881 – 1965)
Born in London. Her father wrote novels and, said Eleanor, "had a way of turning such occasions as Christmas, birthdays, holidays and parties into fairy tales." Typed her own stories and poems from the age of seven.

RUMER GODDEN (1907 –)
Born in England but spent her childhood in India. Often writes of her life there – the heat, the exotic plants, the snakes, the birds and the Indian people she knew. Sometimes writes with her sister, Jon.

MICHAEL ROSEN (1946 –)
Lives in London. A very funny man. Writes poetry, gives talks to school children and appears on television. Likes meatballs, tea, lentils, raisins, wearing cord trousers, staying up late and riding on red London buses. Describes himself as "a big hairy creature".

VERNON SCANNELL (1922 –)
Has been a soldier, a teacher and a resident school poet. Now has a Civil List pension from the government so that he doesn't have to work – except at writing his poems. Likes listening to the radio and watching boxing.

Acknowledgements

Thanks are due to the following publishers, agents and authors for permission to reprint the material indicated.

Every effort has been made to trace copyright but if any omissions have been made please let us know in order that we may put it right in the next edition.

George Allen & Unwin for 'Centipede's Song' by Roald Dahl from *James and the Giant Peach*.
Andre Deutsch for 'If You Don't Put Your Shoes On . . .' by Michael Rosen from *Mind Your Own Business*.
The Lord Alfred Douglas Literary Estate for 'The Shark' by Lord Alfred Douglas. Reprinted by permission.
Granada Publishing Ltd. for 'Hist Whist' by e.e. cummings from *The Complete Poems 1910 – 1962* by e.e. cummings.
Harper & Row, Publishers Inc. for 'About the Teeth of Sharks' by John Ciardi from *You Read to Me, I'll Read to You*, John Ciardi, J. B. Lippincott Co. Copyright © 1962 by the Curtis Publishing Co. Copyright © 1962 by John Ciardi. Reprinted by permission.
David Higham Associates Ltd. for 'Bedtime' by Eleanor Farjeon from *Silver Sand and Snow*, Michael Joseph; 'Mixed Brews' by Clive Sansom from *The Golden Unicorn*, Clive Sansom, Methuen.
Mrs. W. M. Horsbrugh for 'The Train to Glasgow', 'The Cake', 'The Cobbler's Shop', and 'Night Bears'. Reprinted by permission.
Marion Lines for 'Car Breakers' from *Tower Blocks – Poems for City Children* © Marion Lines.
Leslie Norris for 'The Traffic Light'.
Vernon Scannell for 'Sweet Song' from *A First Poetry Book*, O.U.P., compiled by John Foster, 1979.
Shufunotomo Co. Ltd. for 'Hurry Home' by Leonard Clark from *Here and There*.
Mrs. A. M. Walsh for 'Bus to School' by John Walsh from *Roundabout by the Sea*, John Walsh, O.U.P.
World's Work Ltd. for 'What is Red? What is Grey?' by Mary O'Neill from *Hailstones and Halibut Bones*, Mary O'Neill. Reprinted by permission.
Viking Penguin Inc. for 'Prayer of the Ox'. 'Prayer of the Little Ducks' from *Prayers from the Ark* by Carmen Bernos de Gasztold. Translated by Rumer Godden. Copyright 1947, 1955 by Editions du Cloitre. English text Copyright 1962 by Rumer Godden.

We are grateful to the following for assistance in providing photographs: Mary Evans Picture Library pp. 11, 12 & 30; Mansell Collection p. 16; J. Allan Cash Ltd. p. 31; BBC Hulton Picture Library p. 47.